MW00876928

SIMONE BILES

Women in Sports

MARY HERTZ SCARBROUGH

Rourke
Educational Media

A Division of
Carson Dellosa
Education

Before Reading: *Building Background Knowledge and Vocabulary*

Building background knowledge can help children process new information and build upon what they already know. Before reading a book, it is important to tap into what children already know about the topic. This will help them develop their vocabulary and increase their reading comprehension.

Questions and Activities to Build Background Knowledge:

1. Look at the front cover of the book and read the title. What do you think this book will be about?
2. What do you already know about this topic?
3. Take a book walk and skim the pages. Look at the table of contents, photographs, captions, and bold words. Did these text features give you any information or predictions about what you will read in this book?

Vocabulary: *Vocabulary Is Key to Reading Comprehension*

Use the following directions to prompt a conversation about each word.

*   Read the vocabulary words.
*   What comes to mind when you see each word?
*   What do you think each word means?

Vocabulary Words:
*   all-around
*   circuit
*   compulsory
*   dominance
*   elite
*   vault

During Reading: *Reading for Meaning and Understanding*

To achieve deep comprehension of a book, children are encouraged to use close reading strategies. During reading, it is important to have children stop and make connections. These connections result in deeper analysis and understanding of a book.

 Close Reading a Text

During reading, have children stop and talk about the following:

*   Any confusing parts
*   Any unknown words
*   Text to text, text to self, text to world connections
*   The main idea in each chapter or heading

Encourage children to use context clues to determine the meaning of any unknown words. These strategies will help children learn to analyze the text more thoroughly as they read.

When you are finished reading this book, turn to the next-to-last page for **After Reading Questions** and an **Activity**.

TABLE **OF** CONTENTS

LIFE-CHANGING EVENTS

One rainy day changed the life of six-year-old Simone Biles forever. Her day care class was supposed to visit a farm. Because of the weather, they went to a tumbling gym instead.

Coaches at the gym noticed Simone imitating gymnastics moves done by girls in their teens. Soon, she was enrolled in gymnastics classes twice a week.

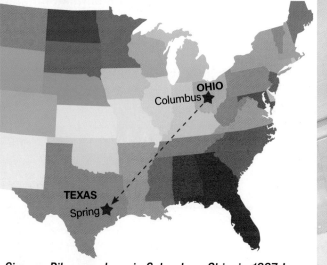

Simone Biles was born in Columbus, Ohio, in 1997. In 2000, she moved to Spring, Texas.

Better Later Than Never

According to Simone, many top gymnasts begin tumbling classes by age three. She was driven by her love of a challenge and a *"fierce drive"* to prove herself.

Simone Biles displays her medal at the 2016 Olympics.

Something else happened when Simone was six. Her grandparents, Ron and Nellie Biles, adopted her and her younger sister, Adria.

Grandma and Grandpa were now Mom and Dad. "Adria and I were finally and forever home."

Ron, Nellie, and Adria Biles cheer in the stands at the 2016 Olympics.

LEAPING INTO COMPETITION

Young Simone was exceptionally strong, and she loved the challenges her coaches gave her. She quickly moved up through several gymnastics levels.

For each level, she had to prove she had mastered the **compulsory** skills. Beginning in level seven, gymnasts can add optional moves to the required ones.

compulsory (kuhm-PUHL-sur-ee): required

Women's Gymnastics Events

Balance Beam

Floor

Vault

Uneven Bars

9

By 2011, Simone was an **elite** junior gymnast, among the best young gymnasts in the United States. But Simone suffered a huge disappointment that year. She wasn't chosen for the U.S. National Team. Thirteen girls were chosen. She was number fourteen on the list. Simone said it "put an ache in my heart and doubts in my mind."

elite (i-LEET): the best of a class or group

Simone placed third in the junior women's all-around competition at the 2012 National Championships.

Tough Lessons

Simone eventually realized that not making the team in 2011 taught her something important. "A person can only fail if they stop trying, if they refuse to pick themselves up and try harder."

Simone was junior champion at the 2012 Secret U.S. Classic.

By the time Simone was 14 years old, she was practicing 25–30 hours a week. But she didn't think that was enough to reach her goals. She made the decision to be homeschooled to allow more time for gymnastics practice.

Sometimes she still faltered, but her sacrifices paid off. Simone hasn't lost the **all-around** title in a competition since 2013.

all-around (awl-uh-ROUND): a competition where gymnasts perform on every piece of equipment

Simone joined Team USA for the 2016 Olympic Games. She was going to Rio De Janeiro, Brazil! Despite all her hard work, sometimes she feared she wouldn't be ready.

The team competition came first. Simone was the only team member who competed in all four events of the competition, but everyone on the team helped win the gold medal.

Girls Just Wanna Have Fun

As she prepared for the Olympics, Simone reminded herself that she always did better if she remembered to have fun. She was *"determined to enjoy every minute."*

Simone poses during the final floor competition.

The team gave itself the nickname "The Final Five."

Simone and Aly Raisman, her friend and teammate, represented Team USA in the individual all-around competition. Simone  finished first in everything except the uneven bars. She won the gold medal, and Raisman took the silver.

In the following days, Simone earned additional gold medals for the **vault** and floor events and a bronze for the balance beam competition.

vault (vawlt): a gymnastics event using a springboard and vaulting table

Left to right: Aliya Mustafina of Russia, Simone Biles of USA, and Aly Raisman of USA

Simone prepares for the balance beam competition at the 2019 U.S. Gymnastics Championships.

Simone took a break from gymnastics in 2017. When she returned to the gymnastics **circuit**, she resumed her winning streak. In 2018, she won the U.S. Gymnastics Championship in every event, as well as the all-around title. In the 2019 competition, she won gold medals in every event except uneven bars, where she placed third.

circuit (SUR-kit): a number or series of activities (such as gymnastics competitions)

Simone continued her **dominance** at the 2018 World Championships. She won gold in all-around, vault, and beam. She won silver in uneven bars and bronze in balance beam.

dominance (DAH-muh-nunce): being in control or the most powerful

At the 2019 worlds, she won five more gold medals, bringing her total number of medals in world competition to 25. With that, Simone became the most decorated gymnast in history.

Best gymnast in the world!

BILES Simone
USA
Age: 22
Qualification Score
1   333

WORLD CHAMPI
RTISTIC
NA
STUT

Simone keeps reaching for new goals, including the goal of competing in more Olympic Games. Her latest move is a triple-double for her floor routine. It is a double back flip with three twists. She is the first woman gymnast to use this move in competition.

What's in a Name?

Simone has four gymnastics moves named after her. There are three moves named the Biles: one for floor exercise, one on the vault, and a balance beam dismount. The Biles II is the double back flip with three twists.

SOARING HIGH

After the 2016 Olympics, Simone took some time off from gymnastics. She wrote a book titled *Courage to Soar: A Body in Motion, A Life in Balance*. She was also a contestant on the popular TV show *Dancing With the Stars*. She and her partner came in fourth place!

Family Ties

Simone's family is very important to her. She dedicated her book to her parents. She wrote:

"To Mom and Dad: Your love keeps me grounded yet gives me the courage to soar toward my dreams."

FOREWORD BY MARY LOU RETTON

COURAGE TO SOAR

A BODY IN MOTION • A LIFE IN BALANCE

SIMONE BILES

WITH *NEW YORK TIMES* BESTSELLING AUTHOR MICHELLE BURFORD

At the U.S. National Gymnastics Championships, Simone wore a teal leotard to show support for abused gymnasts.

In January 2018, Simone posted on Twitter with the hashtag #MeToo. She shared that she, along with 150 other gymnasts and former patients, was abused by a Team USA doctor.

The doctor was found guilty. He will be in prison for the rest of his life. Simone said it's difficult to talk about what happened, but she hopes doing so can help others.

Simone speaks confidently about her success. She wants to help girls feel confident. Simone told a reporter that women are often discouraged from admitting their worth. "But... once you realize you're confident and good at it," she said, "then you're even better at what you do."

Memory Game

Look at the pictures. What do you remember reading on the pages where each image appeared?

Index

After Reading Questions

1. What are three challenges Simone has encountered in her life?

2. Why does Simone believe it's important to acknowledge her success?

3. Did your understanding of what it takes to be one of the greatest athletes in the world change after reading this book? Explain.

4. What gymnastics event would you want to do most? Why?

5. What do you think makes Simone successful and inspiring?

Activity

Simone dedicated her book, *Courage to Soar*, to her parents, Ron and Nellie Biles. If you wrote a book about your life, what are two topics you would focus on? Why? To whom would you dedicate your book?

About the Author

Mary Hertz Scarbrough is in awe of Simone Biles's artistry, strength, dedication, and success—particularly since she herself never mastered a basic cartwheel. Fortunately, her editors have never required her to do one. Instead,

she happily researches and writes from her home in South Dakota.

www.rourkeeducationalmedia.com

Quote source: *Courage to Soar: A Body in Motion, A Life in Balance*, by Simone Biles and Michelle Burford (2015).

PHOTO CREDITS: page 5: ©Petr Toman / Shutterstock, ©Olga Turkas; page 6: ©MIKE BLAKE / NEWSCOM; page 7: ©Katarzyna Bialasiewicz Photographee.eu /Getty Images/iStockphoto; page 9: ©Leonard Zhukovsky / Shutterstock; page 10-11: ©Richard Ulreich / ZUMAPRESS.com/Newscom; page 12: ©Anna Kim / Getty Images/iStockphoto, ©Karen I. Hirsch / ZUMAPRESS/Newscom; page 14-15: ©marchello74; page 15: ©Petr Toman / Shutterstock.com, ©Leonard Zhukovsky / Shutterstock.com; page 16: ©Petr Toman / Shutterstock.com; page 17: ©Leonard Zhukovsky / Shutterstock; page 18-19: © Represented by ZUMA Press, Inc.; page 20-21: ©Marijan Murat / dpa / Newscom; page 21: © Represented by ZUMA Press, Inc.; page 22-23: REUTERS /Newscom, ©Kyodo / Newscom; page 23: ©Melissa J. Perenson / ZUMAPRESS.com / Newscom; page 25: ©Featureflash Photo Agency / Shutterstock; page 26: © Represented by ZUMA Press, Inc.; page 27: ©Brendan McDermid / REUTERS / Newscom; page 28: © Represented by ZUMA Press, Inc.; page 29: ©Yohei Osada / AFLO / Newscom

Edited by: Madison Capitano
Cover and interior design by: Rhea Magaro-Wallace

Library of Congress PCN Data

Simone Biles / Mary Hertz Scarbrough
(Women in Sports)
  ISBN 978-1-73163-825-0 (hard cover)
  ISBN 978-1-73163-902-8 (soft cover)
  ISBN 978-1-73163-979-0 (e-Book)
  ISBN 978-1-73164-056-7 (ePub)
Library of Congress Control Number: 2020930166

Rourke Educational Media
Printed in the United States of America
01-1662011937